8 Steps

to Remember, Recreate, and
Liberate Your Life

....

Gabriela Floriceanu, George Floriceanu,
Carmen Ontanu, Claudia Stroe

Skyhorse Publishing

Skyhorse Publishing books may be purchased in bulk at special discounts for sales promotion, corporate gifts, fund-raising, or educational purposes. Special editions can also be created to specifications. For details, contact the Special Sales Department, Skyhorse Publishing, 307 West 36th Street, 11th Floor, New York, NY 10018 or info@ skyhorsepublishing.com.

Skyhorse® and Skyhorse Publishing® are registered trademarks of Skyhorse Publishing, Inc.®, a Delaware corporation.

Visit our website at www.skyhorsepublishing.com.

10 9 8 7 6 5 4 3 2 1

Library of Congress Cataloging-in-Publication Data is available on file.

Cover design by Jane Sheppard
Cover illustration by Ciprian Udrescu

Hardcover ISBN: 978-1-5107-3049-6

Printed in China

We are all amazing writers of the most important story of all—our own.

Contents

· ·

Part I: Welcome to Your Book

Part II: Start Writing Your Book

Part I

Welcome to Your Book

A Note from the Authors

....

The Book That Wrote Me is a playful interpretation of the idea of authorship. It is generally believed that one needs to convey something of great importance and originality to be considered an author. We do not challenge this belief; what will be challenged and changed through *The Book That Wrote Me* are the ways in which we look at our own lives. Each of our lives are of great importance and they all are, with no exception, unique. If we choose to view life like this, we are all authors—so why not write our own book?

The Book That Wrote Me contains the beautiful, original illustrations of artist Ciprian Udrescu. His mandalas, his visual interpretations of emotions and authorship, give this book—your book— the quality of a work of art. May they help you find joy and inspiration!

Introduction

....

Dear Writer,

Who are you? *Yes, you.* What made you who you are today? Make these questions your guide when allowing this book to help you recreate the most important moments of your life. We can't wait to see who will be waiting on the other side.

We All Have a Story

This story is based on the most significant moments in our lives. It is not the role of this book to decide on those moments. This book is offered to you as a guide to self-expression. It is a set of chapters needing to be written, rewritten, drawn, created, ordered, and reordered—as you have probably already guessed, this book allows you to do anything, as long as you allow yourself to be written.

Why Put Your Life into a Book?

This is a book about *you*. If you have always felt your life is better than a movie, this is your chance to explore it. And if, on the contrary, you feel your life has nothing spectacular in it, this book is all the more for you. Because there is no such thing as a boring or unspectacular life. This world is magnificent because there are over seven billion human stories in it with over seven billion authors. Can you imagine the wonder?

We all have powerful memories in our hearts and minds. Some of them are vivid, while others are almost fading. Memory is a funny thing. Pushed by emotions, it does its job to protect us from what hurts by transforming a powerful memory and reducing it to almost nothing.

This Book Is a Work of Emotions

It can be very difficult for people to talk about their emotions, which is why a piece of paper can be a miraculous tool to help you separate yourself from the subject of your writing or drawing or coloring. Putting an extra layer between you and your past can create a certain degree of distance or detachment. And when detachment occurs, emotions lose their intensity, allowing you to reach a higher level of clarity. In this way, an empty page that you are determined to fill can trigger a change in perspective.

The Book That Wrote Me Is the Result of All Our Experiences

We've all lived through joy and happiness, pain and despair, anger and ecstasy, disappointment and regret. We know how hard it can be to understand these emotions and figure out what triggers them deep inside ourselves. Have you ever been enraged by a certain behavior that doesn't seem to bother anyone else? Or felt negatively affected by a situation considered absolutely banal by others? These emotions can embarrass us and make us feel even more resentful each time they come on until we become prisoners—not of our past, but of our past emotions. Facts are no longer just facts. Choked underneath mixed emotions, events become constructs that can slow us down and determine our present and future emotional reactions to life.

Let's Deconstruct Our Memories!

Let's do it in a creative, beautiful, and colorful way. Give yourself a moment of peace now to think about what you could write or draw about. It could be about something that was left unsolved or something that no longer makes sense; it could be about a deep regret or a great moment of courage; about times of personal hell or times that felt like heaven. It could be about a person who always stood by you or about someone who rocketed through your life yet made a big impact. Pay attention to the voice that says *Hey! That part was interesting!*

And Now, Begin *The Book That Wrote Me*

Take a pen or pencil and write down eight key moments of your life. Write them down at the start of your book as they come to you, regardless of their order. You may change their order before you start working on your book, or introduce a new moment that seems more important than another one already on your list; just make sure it is an honest choice and not a way to run away from a tough memory. Even if you identify a memory you can't or won't put in your book, put it aside as a note. Simply identifying it is a big step forward. You will know what to do with it when the time is right.

After you feel your list is done, start your book with any of the eight moments. Ponder on the moment you choose. Bring it back into your memory. Think about it and feel it through. Stay in it for as long as you need and then give it a title. You must remember that there are no right or wrong choices. Write down the details of that moment that first come to your mind: people, places, dreams, emotions, significance. You can be sure that moment taught you something about yourself—wouldn't it be great to find out what? Maybe your discovery won't be instantaneous, but you will have your book to re-read as often as you want. It will surprise you every time.

To help you correctly identify your emotions and feelings linked to a certain event in your life, we preface each chapter with a short introduction about a single emotion. You will find out more about joy and happiness, anger, sadness, fear, trust, shame, surprise, and love. These are some of the main emotions and feelings that both bless and plague our lives. They can be sources of knowledge, insight, balance, and healing. At the same time, they can be sources of pain, entrapment, and belittlement. Every emotion is caused by an event or a set of events that add up to the infinite fabric of our lives. Some of these events stand out. Search for those inside of you and bring them back to life in your book.

It is not necessary to write or draw about a moment linked to the emotion presented in the introduction of each chapter. You can choose as many happy moments as you want; or as many moments of sadness or anger as you feel like, if they make it on your eight-moment list.

Don't censor yourself in any way. Use the information we give you as nothing more than a guide.

All that you need for this book is already in your mind and heart: you know all the facts and you felt all the emotions and feelings. Write it all down in a natural, relaxed way, the way you feel it, as much as you feel it. And at the end, you will own a written and colorful account of what impacted you, made you happy, tore you apart, inspired you, and made you who you are today. What a precious thing!

User Guide

....

The book you are holding is about to become your creation; *your* book, the book of the moment you're in now. We invite you to choose eight key moments of your life. These moments should be the eight most defining, life-changing events you've experienced in your life thus far. And then we invite you to freely recreate them in the pages of this book. *The Book That Wrote Me* contains exactly eight chapters, each holding a set of different pages and each prefaced by an introduction describing one emotion. These eight emotions—joy/ happiness, anger, sadness, fear, trust, shame, surprise, and love—are meant to give you a brief tour into the fascinating world of our hearts. They are not intended to create a predefined structure of your eight-moment list, so feel free to choose your moments as you will, connected to any emotion that spontaneously springs to your mind.

If you've already shuffled through this book a bit, you will have noticed that it is an interesting collection of pages; some of them are lined, meant for writing (for any kind of text, depending on your inspiration); some of them are blank—we encourage you to use these for drawing or scrapbooking; and mandalas for coloring, once you decide which one of the set of eight best fits each chapter of your life.

Thus, every important moment of your life will be remembered, relived, and, in the end, recreated. Remember that there are no right or wrong choices, just natural, spontaneous, and genuine choices, those that you feel come from deep within you. It doesn't matter if you use too much of a particular color; or if there are too many love-related moments or family-related moments on your list; or too few; or none. This book is meant to help you remember and re-center your life, important moment by important moment, in the most relevant way *for you*.

Don't let other people's expectations influence your choices. Use the time you spend on your book being true to yourself.

Before you start, make sure you have plenty of pencils, pens, and crayons on hand. You don't want to stop right in the middle of an inspired moment to go to the nearest shop; but if that happens, don't worry. It probably means it is not yet time to write or draw or work on that particular memory in that particular way. And most importantly, trust yourself as you write your book. You are surely the best one for the job!

About Mandalas

....

In Hindu and Buddhist symbolism, the mandala is considered a sacred concentric structure that represents the universe. The word *mandala* means "circle" or "center" in old Sanskrit and is considered a geometrical shape with no beginning and no ending. Mandalas are believed to reproduce development patterns in the universe.

Nowadays, many people have discovered the relaxing, structuring quality of mandalas. Founder of analytical psychology Carl Jung famously used mandalas in his work with his patients. He considered the possibility that mandalas have the potential to rearrange the personality, offering a new centering in moments of disorientation.

With its circular shape, a mandala favors relaxation, a creative manifestation of inner structure and healing. Its pattern is positive and potentially infinite. It starts from a center and develops in all directions in a countless number of possibilities. Coloring a mandala can be a great way to improve your state of mind. Many therapists consider it a great way to achieve peace of mind, self-centering, creative liberation of stress, and self-expression.

In this book, you will find eight beautiful mandalas. Choose the one you find suitable for each chapter and color it with the intention of self-discovery, fun, and healing. They will become simple yet powerful expressions of your current being.

We all have the right to be the authors of our lives. We have an infinite power to create, regardless of how we manifest it. We may not all be amazing writers or visual artists; or at least we are not all meant to receive such public confirmations. Yet we all are, without a doubt, the brilliant authors of a unique story—our own.

Good luck!

The Authors

Part II

Start Writing Your Book

"Fill your paper with the breathings of your heart." —William Wordsworth

Write down eight of the most important moments of your life. Order is unimportant.

1.   5.

2.   6.

3.   7.

4.   8.

chapter 1

Joy and Happiness

Name of Event: _____

Age When Event Occurred: _____

About Joy and Happiness

. . . .

"What are you doing, Happy?" asked Joy.
"I'm chasing!" Happiness replied. "What are you doing, Joy?"
"I am," said Joy, and smiled with her heart.

Let's take a tour of the complex and mysterious world of emotions. *The Book That Wrote Me* is essentially a book of emotions, so we will preface each chapter with introductory text on one emotion to help you reconnect with what you felt in each important moment. You will read about joy and happiness, anger, sadness, fear, trust, shame, surprise, and love. Most of these are considered basic emotions, and they are the primary emotional responses of a human being in any given situation. When more basic emotions occur together or in a very short period of time, we enter the world of secondary emotions. And when an emotion endures, we are talking about feelings. But let's not go into details just yet. Let's stick to the plan and talk about the first two emotions on our list. Let's start by meeting joy and happiness.

You've experienced joy. You know its warm, sunny, velvety texture. A distinction should be made from the beginning between joy and happiness. It is no coincidence that most languages have two almost perfect synonyms for the same concept. Almost. Because there is a deep difference between the two. Joy is an emotion constructed internally. It is joy that wise men feel who have made peace with the world. It is joy that small children manifest so spontaneously. Joy is not externally motivated and is independent of any external event. Joy has to do with balance and inner peace.

Happiness on the other hand is an emotion built on external input. It is our emotional reaction to an event that we perceive as positive. Happiness means something different to each of us, which is why people feel happy for such different reasons. Have you ever wondered why happiness never seems to last? You work your whole life to buy your dream house because attaining it promises eternal bliss. You train for years to win a contest; it becomes your life goal and victory promises to bring all the happiness in the world. We promise ourselves that once we find true love—usually defined as someone else, someone who is "right" for us—we would be forever happy. And yet, once we move into our dream house, win the so-desired trophy, find the partner that fulfills our needs, happiness fades away. And sometimes it does so frustratingly fast. So, what do we do? We move on to our next external objective that promises the elusive lost paradise of happiness.

This would be a good moment for you to ask yourself *when* you felt happy and *why*. Pay attention to this *why*: happiness is always connected to a *why*. You need a reason to be happy. And then search for a moment when you felt joy. It is not that hard to differentiate between the two. Have you ever had a perfect moment for no reason at all? That was joy. Joy has no *why*. Joy just *is* and even though it also goes away, chocked underneath our human fears and tears, joy is like a mountain top. Once you get there and have seen and felt it all, you never forget it. You may find yourself at the base of the mountain again, overwhelmed with so many other emotions (you will read about them later on), but the view on top will stay with you forever. You know it is there, you know what it feels like, and you know it is attainable.

Even though they are sisters, joy and happiness are different in another way, which makes them both perfect just the way they are for whomever finds them in their heart at a certain point in their lives. To put it simply, joy is passive and happiness is active. To be more accurate, we could say that joy has a tendency to be passive, and happiness is more prone to being active. What does that mean?

By being linked to external objectives, happiness forces us to go out there and do it. Happiness teaches us to be determined, to define our goals and dreams, to go full speed into whatever life has to offer. Okay, we may change our goals along the way, as we may find them less satisfactory as time goes by, but there is a better, fuller, more experienced "us" with every landmark we conquer along the path to the land of the happy. Happiness is the perfect search for the doer.

Joy, on the other hand, is still. It just smiles and needs no more. Its power is immense since it manages to center and make us content with what is, thus detaching us from a concrete quest. And it is joy that gives us mental and emotional rest, as we all need an occasional break from the tireless quest for happiness.

We will not go into the philosophical analysis and debate that has surrounded joy and happiness for thousands of years. We just want to underline the immense importance of these emotions. Whether internally or externally motivated, it is joy and happiness that all humans crave and search for. They are such arduous objectives and desires that we can safely call them two of the engines of human evolution. If people didn't have happiness and joy to search for, where would we be as a civilization, as a race?

Happiness and joy are emotional ideals. They give us a perspective, a vision of possible accomplishment. It is hard to find them; it is even harder to hold onto them. But maybe that's the point. If we had happiness or joy all the time, we wouldn't get the chance to meet the rest of the emotional pack. And they are all intense, smart, amazing teachers!

Close your eyes and immerse yourself in the moment you want to recreate. Pick up all that comes to mind—colors, sounds, people, smells, tastes, dreams, emotions—then take a pen and start expressing them in writing. It doesn't matter how or where on the page. No two people express their emotions the same way. You could write single words or short lines, poem-like clusters, or, if inspired, you could write as you would in a diary! Summon your memories, relive the moment in your mind, and let it pour out on the pages.

Is the defining moment you chose for this chapter linked to color? To shape? To textures of any kind? This is where it can all be recreated. Use whatever tools you like: colored pencils, crayons, fabrics, photos, clippings, anything that you feel can help you express your emotions linked to this defining moment. Don't let your mind dictate what looks good or not. That's not the point. The point is to obtain an expression of your inner landscape connected to the moment you chose.

Color this mandala in the shade(s) that best represent your defining moment. Don't feel compelled to go for the most conventional color. Make the choice that feels most genuine by allowing yourself to pick the color(s) you feel drawn to.

chapter 2

Anger

Name of Event: _____

Age When Event Occurred: _____

About Anger

....

"There are two types of fire," the old man said. "One burns and destroys, the other one warms and gives life."

"Which one am I?" asked the young man.

"Both," said the old man.

It is very easy to think of anger in negative terms. Anger is bad. Anger can cause anger; fights; violence. It often exhausts us and sometimes leaves us filled with shame and remorse. However, anger is seldom, if ever, just a negative emotion with a lot of damage potential.

Let's look at anger from another perspective.

How do we react to injustice? To abuse? To intrusion in our private space? With anger. Simply put, anger is the emotion that signals, "That's it!" When tolerance ends, anger begins. Since injustice, abuse, and intrusion are all very subjective (think about how culturally determined justice can be: the same action considered just in one culture can be considered totally unjust to another), it is not always easy to tell if our moments of anger are really justified. But this is the trouble with moments of anger—they can occur in an instant and leave little to no room for reason.

In many ways, anger is like fire. An emotional fire. Something that can go up in flares in an instant and burn everything in its wake, leaving behind terrible consequences, or something that can start small, signal danger, and be put out just in time. Anger is an enormous force that can do a lot of damage, but it can also engender positive action and change, purify and help. Just like fire.

There is probably not a soul in this world that has not experienced the immense diversity and depth of this emotion. Have you ever felt annoyed? Agitated? Irritated? Frustrated? Offended? Exasperated? Outraged? Vengeful? Enraged? Furious? Livid? Well, the good news is that you are very much a normal human being for feeling all of these mild to acute forms of anger.

Try and bring back a moment of anger. Was it you being angry? Was someone else angry with you? Why? What was the reason? With anger, things are rarely simple because there are so many unconscious triggers in our minds and hearts. Picture a young child being mocked for showing atypical behavior. He/she first feels shame. Then he/she feels exposed and vulnerable; his/her private comfortable space has been invaded by what he/she perceives as unjust reactions and he/she will experience anger. What the young child *does* with that anger is essential. Will he/she use it to generate change in him/herself and in others? Will he/she use it to get him/ herself to continue to act as him/herself, no matter what? Or will he/she use it to lash out and inflict some sort of punishment on others? Arguably, the young child's reaction to anger depends a lot on his/her personality and on his/her early parental relationships. Why? Because in early childhood, we learn a lot. Including how we feel in certain situations, what makes us feel happy, sad, or angry. And if our parents had the inspiration to capture our moments in a conversation, tempt us and engage us in dialogue, make us say how we feel and why—oh, what a tremendous gain! For the child in us will begin to trust in him/herself and in others and will begin to correctly identify and express his/her emotions.

In the case of a six-year-old boy going through many rough childhood experiences in a short period of time (his parents' divorce, moving out, starting his first year of school), the boy experienced severe feelings of anger that he sometimes could not contain. He would lash out at his mother and offend her. But then, one day, the mother had an idea after a bruising episode that left her in tears. She told her son a story of a little boy who lived with his mother. The mother loved him dearly and tried everything in her power to raise him to become a good man. She was always there for him, even when the little boy would misbehave and hurt her. She knew her baby was in pain and loved him even more so the pain would go away and leave him happy. Obviously, the story was a reinterpretation of the mother and son's situation. Instead of scolding the boy and escalating the spiral of anger and hurt, she chose to use a story to make the moment pleasant for the boy and offer a feeling of detachment from the recent fight.

At first, the boy didn't react. After listening to the story, he went to his room to play. But after ten minutes, he rushed into his mother's arms, crying and apologizing for his behavior. They had their first heart-to-heart moment in a very long time. The mother used the moment to get her son to open up and express his feelings of pain and anger. To our knowledge, this episode helped the mother and son duo tremendously. So you see, the more open we are to learning about and understanding our emotions, the better we can identify and manage our emotional states and express them.

Going back to anger, it has probably been with human beings since the beginning of time. In its most acute forms, it is one of the most intense, impulsive, and hardest emotions to resist. Most psychologists consider it a secondary emotion, meaning that the onset of anger is usually preceded by another emotion. You need to feel sad or frightened, for example, before anger sets in as a reaction to the former. But beyond any analysis and attempt to understand anger with our minds, we recommend looking at anger with the eye of your heart. Know that where anger shows, pain or shame has long lived. Show compassion. Show as much understanding as you can. Don't fight anger with anger, if you can. And if your moments of anger have left wounds and bruises, maybe it's time to let it all out. Remember. Reinterpret. Heal.

Close your eyes and immerse yourself in the moment you want to recreate. Pick up all that comes to mind—colors, sounds, people, smells, tastes, dreams, emotions—then take a pen and start expressing them in writing. It doesn't matter how or where on the page. No two people express their emotions the same way. You could write single words or short lines, poem-like clusters, or, if inspired, you could write as you would in a diary! Summon your memories, relive the moment in your mind, and let it pour out on the pages.

_____

_____

_____

_____

_____

_____

_____

_____

_____

_____

_____

_____

_____

_____

Is the defining moment you chose for this chapter linked to color? To shape? To textures of any kind? This is where it can all be recreated. Use whatever tools you like: colored pencils, crayons, fabrics, photos, clippings, anything that you feel can help you express your emotions linked to this defining moment. Don't let your mind dictate what looks good or not. That's not the point. The point is to obtain an expression of your inner landscape connected to the moment you chose.

Color this mandala in the shade(s) that best represent your defining moment. Don't feel compelled to go for the most conventional color. Make the choice that feels most genuine by allowing yourself to pick the color(s) you feel drawn to.

chapter 3

Sadness

Name of Event: _____

Age When Event Occurred: _____

About Sadness

....

"I'm so sad . . ." whispered the young woman.

"Don't fear sadness," the old man said. *"It will help you find your soul."*

Sadness is the Stradivarius of all emotions. It has the amazing ability to make us turn inward, silence the outside noise, and focus on our heart. Sadness is connected to the feeling of loss. We have all lost something or someone; sometimes we may feel like we've lost everything. Losing a job, house, friend, or family member can make us lose our sense of clarity, joy, or hope. In these moments of loss, our heart vibrates. We rediscover it in our chest, playing different notes than those of joy. Sadness can create emotional masterpieces because there is beauty and intensity in it. It's the music of our heart, played in a minor key.

The healthiest way to face sadness is to accept it when it comes, let it run its course, and find a way to move on. It can be difficult to do this alone for two reasons. One is that sadness has a tendency to settle in and stay, almost as an addiction. You can become trapped inside your mind and heart, inside a time bubble where past and present mingle and memories create a hard-to-escape, bittersweet, beautiful secondary reality. In this case, people around you can help you pull yourself out of it and live! The second reason we can't face sadness alone is because, as we have said, sadness indicates loss. As long as we feel that empty space in our soul, we will continue to go back to that black hole of loss. When this goes on for too long, a guide—a therapist or a gifted friend—could help us change our perspective on loss and figure out a way to close it or put something else in its place to stop it from draining precious life energy out of us.

Like any other emotion, sadness is an early friend in our lives. Children feel it early; it accompanies the natural process of separation from their mother. They discover that separation exists and they need to find ways to cope with it. In a less intellectual society, arguably things would unfold in a natural, unforced, unanalytical way. Children would be allowed to separate; experience a degree of sadness; discover their inner world in the process; get accustomed to sadness as a part of their normal emotional being and seek help if necessary. In our society, the naturalness of this process is a bit lost because our culture is so contingent on the constant pursuit of happiness. We fight our natural feelings of pain and loss and sadness, and when the signs of sadness present themselves in our children, we try to do the same for them. They should have more toys; more fun activities; more shows; more trips; more knowledge. They should be happy. Always happy. We, in our assumed roles as parents, need to ensure our children's happiness as a way to ensure our own.

Happiness is an emotional dependence based on outside factors. If we raise our children to be dependent on outside stimuli for their own happiness, we deny them the early path to joy. And the road to joy goes through pain. And loss. And yes, sadness. Remember, sadness helps us find our soul. A child will connect to his/her inner essence the moment he discovers he/she is singular. A being of his/her own right.

By the way, do you remember? That moment, when looking at your mother made you a bit sad? When you wanted to seclude for a while and explore a surprising, mild, bittersweet sensation that you could not name then, but found out later it is called melancholy? When you felt that vibrant place in your chest and discovered it for the first time? That is a precious moment and a precious memory. It was the moment when your inner journey began and you unconsciously began to wonder, *who am I?* This question is for you to answer, and it is a lifelong pursuit.

Let us help you a bit with what we believe you are *not*. You are not your loss. What we lose was never ours to keep. Loss indicates empty places in our beings; places that we fill with external input. When the external input is torn away from you, your inner fabric hurts and demands that something else is put back in its place. Whenever possible, try to understand what exactly you miss the most in what you have lost. The love? The security? The trust? The smile that signaled warmth? If there is one thing that we can learn from loss every single time, it is that whatever we feel we have lost is already inside of us. Loss helps us find and regain lost parts of ourselves. Our capacity to love; to feel safe; to give.

So, trust sadness. Allow it to take you deep into your soul, find the meaning of your loss, and fill that perceived empty space with the breathings of your own heart.

Close your eyes and immerse yourself in the moment you want to recreate. Pick up all that comes to mind—colors, sounds, people, smells, tastes, dreams, emotions—then take a pen and start expressing them in writing. It doesn't matter how or where on the page. No two people express their emotions the same way. You could write single words or short lines, poem-like clusters, or, if inspired, you could write as you would in a diary! Summon your memories, relive the moment in your mind, and let it pour out on the pages.

Is the defining moment you chose for this chapter linked to color? To shape? To textures of any kind? This is where it can all be recreated. Use whatever tools you like: colored pencils, crayons, fabrics, photos, clippings, anything that you feel can help you express your emotions linked to this defining moment. Don't let your mind dictate what looks good or not. That's not the point. The point is to obtain an expression of your inner landscape connected to the moment you chose.

Color this mandala in the shade(s) that best represent your defining moment. Don't feel compelled to go for the most conventional color. Make the choice that feels most genuine by allowing yourself to pick the color(s) you feel drawn to.

chapter 4

Fear

Name of Event: _____

Age When Event Occurred: _____

About Fear

Thank you, Fear, for leading us thus far. Just know your place!

....

"I've always been afraid," said the little girl.

"Of what?" asked the older woman.

"Of dangers of any kind," said the little girl.

"Can we determine danger?" asked the older woman.

We have seen that anger is connected to perceived injustice and sadness is connected to the idea of loss. In the case of fear, the connection leads to the idea of danger. What is danger? This is a very personal question. It is very difficult to differentiate between the subjective and objective essence of danger. What is dangerous to me may not be dangerous to you and vice versa. Sure, there are moments when we can all agree danger is present: an obvious attack or an accident; however, what we experience determines our perception of danger.

Fear is the emotion our brain generates to keep us safe. It has always been paramount to our survival. We all have a collective, inherent sense of danger. For thousands and thousands of years, mankind has accumulated experiences in which danger occurred, fear was felt, and man was compelled to act. This is how the fight-or-flight pattern was established in our genes. Generation after generation, men felt fear and either chose to stay and face the perceived danger, or turn around and run for their lives. Another reaction to immediate danger is called the "freeze" instinct. Basically, our mind and body correlate and generate the necessary response for us to face danger in the best possible way—accelerated heartbeat, tense muscles, fast breathing. If an animal charges, a vehicular impact is imminent, a thief is in our house—the urgency of these situations makes our brain choose one of our response routes of fight, flight, or freeze.

These ancient fears that we each carry within our every cell ensure that when immediate and objective danger strikes, we are equipped with the right reactions that have the most potential to save our lives. In this way, fear is positive. It is an alert, instinctual, and ever-present lifeguard we should be so thankful for. But then, as with all emotions, fear has its dark side. The side where our perception of danger is distorted and fear becomes an abnormal burden and consumer of energy. These are the fears of our everyday lives, which are connected to subjective dangers and to our experiences within our family, groups, and communities: fear of rejection, of not belonging, of failure, of success, fear of being hurt, fear of commitment, of involvement—and the list could go on for pages. We fear spiders, birds, bugs, feathers; we fear love, rejection, abandonment. We fear potential futures and potential hurts. And so, we become prisoners of our fears, which can take over our lives and push us to live safe. Oh, so safe.

There are two types of fear that we all experience, which shape our existence and determine the quality of our lives: the fear of death and the fear of love. The fear of death is a paradoxical emotion. When experiencing an exacerbated fear of death, we often stop living our lives to the fullest. In our obsessive need to make sure we conserve our safety, we miss opportunities that could enrich our lives and help us develop and grow as human beings. As unlikely as it sounds, coming to terms with the truth of our mortality is the path to a more enriched and fulfilling life.

The fear of love is an early companion for most people. We learn to fear love in experiences where love becomes hurtful. As children, we love our parents unconditionally. The trouble is that our parents are not kids anymore, so they manifest love the way life taught them to; that is why, from very early on, we learn to withdraw, to close up and inhibit this amazing capacity to love. We learn that we are vulnerable. We associate love with vulnerability and pain and can end up fearing it. We live our lives craving love and yet we subconsciously run away from it. It is not hard to become aware of our fear to love. It is harder to move past it and will ourselves to open our hearts to love. It is our hope that this book will help you do just that.

Determining our fears is not easy. When asked, nearly everyone will give you their most common and comfortable-to-admit fear: "Sure, I'm afraid of flying," "of my dad," "of speaking in public." Yet fear goes further down. In the examples we just mentioned, it is reasonable to translate the fear of flying into fear of giving up control; the fear of our father into fear of judgement or rejection; the fear of speaking in public into fear of failure and judgement.

Ask yourself this question now: *what am I afraid of?* Take a pen and paper and write down your fears as they first come to you. Don't try to understand anything yet. Then take that list and decompose your fears. Don't link your fears to outside factors like planes, people, or bugs. Take your fears inward. Ask yourself, *why do I fear this?* Most of the time you will see that your fear is not objectively determined. It is not the outside world that causes you to be afraid, but your inner emotional world, your own past, experiences, and interactions that really determine your fears. And sometimes, they are not real. They are simply traps or doors closed to unlived potential and life's beauty. Our mind says, "if you're afraid, don't go there." And most of the time we really don't go there, even if "there" might just be the best thing that could happen to us.

In this world of dualism, we all try balancing the positive and the negative aspects of our lives to work in our favor. When negativity strikes, just like a battery we try to spark our positive energy and move forward. It's just the same with fear. The downside of fear, with its strong emotional insecurities and conditionings, has an immense potential upside, if we allow ourselves to face that fear. Wherever a big fear lies, you could just find your life's purpose. The thing you could be great at; amazing; the thing that you were born to do. Are you afraid of speaking in public? You might actually have a *voice.* And by that we mean a message and the power to give it to people.

Let us tell you a story about fear. It is the story of a very creative young man who was afraid to face the world as himself. He had this conviction that he was weak, weird, and hardly fitting in under any circumstance or context. He was afraid to open his mouth and state his opinions because he felt he had none to offer. He felt he was small, unimportant, an immature boy among men. He was afraid of people and of talking to them.

Yet he had a gift of humor; profound yet easy to cope with humor. He never perceived it as anything unusual because it came so naturally to him. Whenever he opened his mouth, people would laugh their heart out. His humor was always connected to particularities of his audience, be it a friend or a group of colleagues.

What he really had was a voice. He was unaware of it, so for most of his youth he hid behind the comfort of an advertising job. Yet life is wise and seldom lets us linger where we don't belong. The young man was soon in a situation where he needed to push his limits and his fears. His financial difficulties made it so he could not afford to say no to anything—so he went for it. He changed his job, became a comedy theater director and later a life coach and trainer. He now sits in front of big crowds and makes people laugh at life. Gives his audience a sense of "okay, if it's funny, it can't really be that hard or serious." And people love him for it. Those people that he dreaded and thought would never give a dime for his opinions actually love him. That's what awaited him on the other side of fear.

If faced, fear can open a path to self-discovery and self-trust. It shows us where our biggest vulnerability lies and also our greatest hidden strength. Allow yourself to explore and admit to your vulnerabilities. Face them. Don't fear fear and it might turn into one of your greatest teachers, a power engine of your personal journey.

Bon courage!

Close your eyes and immerse yourself in the moment you want to recreate. Pick up all that comes to mind—colors, sounds, people, smells, tastes, dreams, emotions—then take a pen and start expressing them in writing. It doesn't matter how or where on the page. No two people express their emotions the same way. You could write single words or short lines, poem-like clusters, or, if inspired, you could write as you would in a diary! Summon your memories, relive the moment in your mind, and let it pour out on the pages.

_____

_____

_____

_____

_____

_____

_____

_____

_____

_____

_____

_____

_____

Is the defining moment you chose for this chapter linked to color? To shape? To textures of any kind? This is where it can all be recreated. Use whatever tools you like: colored pencils, crayons, fabrics, photos, clippings, anything that you feel can help you express your emotions linked to this defining moment. Don't let your mind dictate what looks good or not. That's not the point. The point is to obtain an expression of your inner landscape connected to the moment you chose.

Color this mandala in the shade(s) that best represent your defining moment. Don't feel compelled to go for the most conventional color. Make the choice that feels most genuine by allowing yourself to pick the color(s) you feel drawn to.

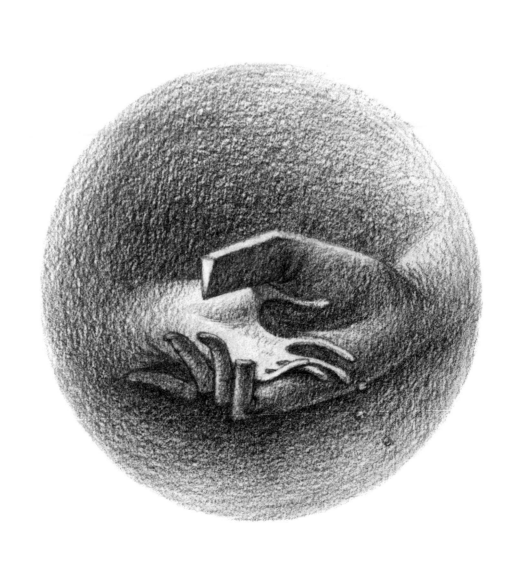

chapter 5

Trust

Name of Event: _____

Age When Event Occurred: _____

About Trust

....

"Where does trust start?" asked the young man.
"Where you begin. In yourself," the old man replied.

Trust is one emotion that links back to you in almost every way. Trust is about perception; your level of trust in everything and anything that surrounds you reflects your perception of reality. And perception is built on experience, particularly early life experience. And this brings us back again to childhood.

A newborn baby has no concept of trust. A baby simply *is*. He/she is unconcerned and unburdened with what his/her developing mind will generate in time: personhood, individuality, separation. When unseparated, trust is void of any meaning. Think about the cells in our body. Do you think there is any notion of trust going on between them? Probably not. The concept does not exist because it is not necessary without the awareness of separation.

But, as we have previously discussed, there comes a moment in our lives as conscious beings when we begin to separate from our parents to discover our individuality and question our nature. This is the important and vulnerable moment when we form our alliance with the world. And during this time, our experiences will shape how we see the world. Will we see it as a place of potential, adventure, joy? As a place where we belong? Or will we see it as a dangerous and frightening source of the unknown? The prevailing perception will make us more or less prone to trust—events, others, and life itself.

Ask yourself now, are you a person who trusts? Do you trust others? Are you generally of a suspicious nature? Do you always take precautions no matter what you do? Now, go further back in time and try to see yourself five, ten, fifteen years ago. Were you the same? Some of us begin life full of trust and are lucky enough to keep this wonderful feeling almost untouched. Some of us get hurt. And some of us learn the path of mistrust.

Emotions are not right or wrong. They are simply amazing mirrors of who we were at a certain point in our lives. We may choose to use these mirrors to show us our honest selves. Are we too trusting? Do we do it for real or is it just a way to please others? Are we too untrusting? Would we be willing to take some risks? If so, what would be our reward? If we agree that what goes around comes around, this should be true for trust, too. Basically, when you genuinely trust more, you will probably be seen and appreciated as more trustworthy yourself. Why? Because trust means investing something of yourself in someone else. For free. No hidden agenda. Most people will feel your sense of trust and respond accordingly, because you will have established a very special connection.

Trust is linked to generosity and to love. When we trust someone, we decide to open up and become vulnerable. Even when there is no solid and apparent reason to trust someone, sometimes we take a leap of faith and we decide to trust. Why? Because of our need to reconnect to others. If there is no trust, we are alone. And we are not meant to be alone; we are social beings with an inherent yearning to develop meaningful relationships; to love; to trust. Life is an interesting journey. We begin it with separation so we become aware of ourselves and then we use this awareness and spend our whole life trying to link back and heal this separation. Who says life is easy and logical?

Lack of trust, on the other hand, is linked to fear. Think of the people and situations you don't trust. Lack of trust in your life partner? You are probably afraid of getting hurt. Don't trust a business opportunity? You are probably afraid of being cheated. The golden rule of a balanced life is a balanced attitude. Going to extremes is certainly an enlightening and useful experience (because you get to see how far or deep you can go, you can test your limits), yet be aware that trust or lack of trust are not absolutes. Allow yourself to trust; allow yourself to not trust. And above all, allow yourself to see what both attitudes bring into your life. This is the best way to absorb and balance your level of trust.

Let us give you an example of a man going through a vulnerable stage in his life. He craved a meaningful relationship. Life materialized an opportunity and he met a woman. They instantly bonded, but he had a physical ailment he couldn't accept. He assumed that no woman would really accept it; therefore, no woman would really accept *him*. When she behaved as if there was nothing wrong with him, he could not bring himself to believe that she was genuine, so he began to doubt her. He was in love but his initial wound produced toxic thoughts; in the end, he pushed her away from him. His lack of trust produced a second wound in his soul that caused him to give up the woman he loved. Yet, if he had taken the opportunity to trust her, he may have healed his initial wound and become aware that he is lovable just as he is. This is what trust could have given him.

Trust or lack of trust is connected to your true self. When this emotion springs from deep within you, it is a genuine and very useful guide when making a choice. Remember: trust begins with yourself. Work with yourself, be generous and loving with yourself, and you will learn to trust in yourself, in others, and in life.

Close your eyes and immerse yourself in the moment you want to recreate. Pick up all that comes to mind—colors, sounds, people, smells, tastes, dreams, emotions—then take a pen and start expressing them in writing. It doesn't matter how or where on the page. No two people express their emotions the same way. You could write single words or short lines, poem-like clusters, or, if inspired, you could write as you would in a diary! Summon your memories, relive the moment in your mind, and let it pour out on the pages.

_____

_____

_____

_____

_____

_____

_____

_____

_____

_____

_____

_____

Is the defining moment you chose for this chapter linked to color? To shape? To textures of any kind? This is where it can all be recreated. Use whatever tools you like: colored pencils, crayons, fabrics, photos, clippings, anything that you feel can help you express your emotions linked to this defining moment. Don't let your mind dictate what looks good or not. That's not the point. The point is to obtain an expression of your inner landscape connected to the moment you chose.

Color this mandala in the shade(s) that best represent your defining moment. Don't feel compelled to go for the most conventional color. Make the choice that feels most genuine by allowing yourself to pick the color(s) you feel drawn to.

chapter 6

Shame

Name of Event: _____

Age When Event Occurred: _____

About Shame

"Shame is a soul eating emotion." —C. G. Jung

. . . .

"You want to change?"

"Yes!"

"Then get rid of shame."

We all grow up with a set of expectations regarding our persona. How much of these expectations actually belong to us or are projected onto us by others is a discussion in and of itself. The thing is, in the back of our mind, we all develop an image of ourselves, an ideal that the mind pushes forward as the perfect "I" that would ensure acceptance, appreciation, and ultimately, the so-desired and elusive happiness.

Our problems begin when what we actually are (or perceive ourselves to be) does not match our personal ideal. "I pictured myself already married by the time I turned thirty" is a fragment of the picture-perfect construct of a particular woman who was not married at thirty-seven. She felt ashamed because she thought people would judge her and consider her to be unattractive or not worthy of a man's total commitment. Consequently, she would frequently lie about her age, about her never being married; she subtracted years and added on husbands; or she would totally avoid men she really, really liked, because the idea of having to face her shame was unbearable.

Shame is the pain of our ego; sometimes it is mild and goes away quickly, as it is caused by a singular and contained event that we know we can correct. (Have you ever experienced a bad breath episode? Or a hot day when your deodorant just wasn't up to the job?) At other times, shame can be devastating and make us retreat deeper inside ourselves. Look down. Hide. These are the times when we feel exposed to judgement, and the gap between the perfect construct of our persona and the reality of it is in danger of showing up. In these times of inner pain, be gentle on yourself. If the pressure is too much, it's okay to retreat, but try to understand the source of your pain. Investigate it and put it in the simplest possible words. It could sound like "I'm ashamed because I feel I am uneducated" or "I am ashamed because I feel like a failure" or "I am ashamed because I feel stupid." And then ask yourself: "Is this really so? Am I really uneducated? A failure? Stupid?" Sometimes the answer is yes, and if so, then it's probably time to do something about it. If the answer is no, you might come to realize that you have integrated other people's opinions and standards as your own. If that's the case, maybe it's time to seek and uncover your own standards, those that are beneficial and true to you.

Like any other emotion, shame can be dangerous as well as beneficial. If you allow yourself to dwell in your painful, acute shame for too long, you could become depressed and enter a dangerous zone of self-destructive behavior such as isolating yourself from others to avoid any context that could recreate a vulnerable situation that would expose your reason for shame. This kind of behavior only increases your feelings of inadequacy and does not give you any opportunity to work on the true reason for your shame. The wound of shame can be healed if we courageously open it up and clean it. Not everyone can do this alone. Therapy can be of great help with all of the work and willpower needed to discover how our built-up ideal image puts us to shame—and why we ended up building it anyway. This can lead us out of the shame-caused blockage and help us make a healthy decision: we either give up parts of that construct, as we realize they were never really relevant to our true selves ("I don't need two college degrees to prove I'm smart"), or we push forward to attain that stature that would truly make us proud of ourselves ("Tomorrow I'm going back to college. It's what I'm passionate about and it would enrich my life").

Working to move past our shame can be such a liberating process. We often realize that the really painful judgement was not coming from those around us, but from ourselves. It is *we* who judge ourselves against our expectations. When life pushes us into situations where our self-judgements, which are a form of self-aggression, manifest and hurt us, we must pay attention and *do something about it*. Always pay attention to pain. It is there to ring a bell.

Are you at a party and feel ashamed by your dress? Ask yourself why. Is the dress inappropriate? In what way: too casual, too elegant, too cheap? What does your doubt say about you? Often, others immediately pick up that you are unsure of yourself and your choices and in this way, your self-judgement becomes your worst enemy. You probably know people who can pull themselves off no matter what they wear, say, or do. They can come to a party dressed like crazy and have all the confidence in the world. That's the consequence of self-acceptance. Oh, boy! What a big word: *self-acceptance*. We need to understand that we are not here just to fit into the patterns that many others before us have put in place. Every little thing that singles us out is precious, whether it causes us joy or pain because, as we have seen, underneath every situation that triggers a powerful emotion lies the potential to discover more of ourselves, heal something, and shine a little brighter.

So next time you find yourself in a situation when a shame crisis is about to occur, take a look at the person in front of you or at those around you. Know that they feel shame too—surely for different reasons and in different situations, yet they all have personal ideals to overcome. Ask yourself, *What would I do if he/she admitted his/her shame in front of me?* Would you be amused and sarcastic? Probably not. Your heart would probably go out to that person in understanding, support, and yes—maybe even acceptance. Every time we accept someone's reason for shame, we help a soul heal a little. We all have this amazing capacity to help others find new places of comfort and peace in self-acceptance. And since we are all connected, be sure that when we do that for another, we also help ourselves in the process. We understand. We accept. We change.

Close your eyes and immerse yourself in the moment you want to recreate. Pick up all that comes to mind—colors, sounds, people, smells, tastes, dreams, emotions—then take a pen and start expressing them in writing. It doesn't matter how or where on the page. No two people express their emotions the same way. You could write single words or short lines, poem-like clusters, or, if inspired, you could write as you would in a diary! Summon your memories, relive the moment in your mind, and let it pour out on the pages.

_____

_____

_____

_____

_____

_____

_____

_____

_____

_____

_____

_____

Is the defining moment you chose for this chapter linked to color? To shape? To textures of any kind? This is where it can all be recreated. Use whatever tools you like: colored pencils, crayons, fabrics, photos, clippings, anything that you feel can help you express your emotions linked to this defining moment. Don't let your mind dictate what looks good or not. That's not the point. The point is to obtain an expression of your inner landscape connected to the moment you chose.

Color this mandala in the shade(s) that best represent your defining moment. Don't feel compelled to go for the most conventional color. Make the choice that feels most genuine by allowing yourself to pick the color(s) you feel drawn to.

chapter **7**

Surprise

Name of Event: _____

Age When Event Occurred: _____

About Surprise

....

"What is surprise?"

"The unpredictable teacher of the unknown."

"Surpriiiise!!" is probably the first thing that comes to mind when we try to envision surprise. An intense, sudden, happy moment that puts a smile on our faces, like a surprise birthday party or visit. Taken lightly, surprise seems to be the least life-changing emotion of the ones we have presented so far (unless, of course, you have won the lottery—now, this surprise is bound to change your life). Surprise seems to be a short-lived emotion and doesn't seem to run as deep as sadness or shame or love.

And yet, it is surprise that gets us out of the box. Surprise occurs when something happens outside "life as usual" or "the world as we know it." Both our life experience and our everyday social and cultural environments dictate our understanding of a normal, predictable flow of events. And sometimes, something happens that disrupts our anticipated understanding. At that moment, we are forced to admit to surprise and make adjustments to the way we see the world.

Surprise is a wonderful teacher; a very wise one, even though its teachings aren't always light and easy. It shows us time and time again *that we actually don't know everything and we never stop learning.* There is always something out there that is unpredictable, new, unforeseen, and surprising.

There are many causes for surprise. We will choose to zoom in on the kind of surprise that has the potential to induce deep change. When a friend startles you or a dog barks at you unexpectedly from behind a fence, surprise occurs as an intense emotional wave, yet most likely it all goes back to normal once the source of the startle has been identified. We typically take some personal lessons away from a surprise—even in these mild cases, you learn that your friend can be unpredictable, and you will probably be mentally prepared next time you go by that fence. But let's go to another level of surprise and imagine one of the following scenarios: your parents tell you that you are adopted; or your daughter comes home with her girlfriend and lets you know she is gay; or your beloved asks for a divorce after a period of time that felt like a second honeymoon.

Surprise occurs in each of the aforementioned cases and can have the shattering effect of a massive earthquake. It affects the lives of everyone involved and forces them to take in, absorb, and integrate the consequences. Life as they know it will never be the same. Their understanding of reality will never be the same. Arguably, even though some surprises could be perceived as bad surprises, their effect always leads to some sort of opportunity for improvement.

It is very hard for a child to take in the idea that he or she has no known roots. That his or her life has been what could be perceived as a lie. And yet, that child has the opportunity, often with the help of those around him or her, to appreciate the good fortune of being adopted as an alternative to growing up in a foster home; of being loved and cared for; of having a good life. The wound caused by surprise could teach the lesson of gratitude and acceptance. It is not an easy lesson and it usually takes time to sink in. This kind of surprise can trigger severe anger and major issues of trust—so you see, surprise is a very powerful emotion that can open the door to a lot of emotional turmoil.

It's no wonder you hear people say "I don't like surprises. Nope! Not for me." How many people do you hear saying "I don't like anger?" or "I don't like fear?" Even though these are two overwhelming and potentially harmful emotions, neither of them have the potential to brutally disrupt your worldview as suddenly as surprise.

Surprise seems to function like a reset in certain aspects of our lives. We need surprise to wake us up or make us aware of things that were not, up to the moment of surprise, part of our established vision of our environment. You hardly pay attention to this or that topic or aspect of reality until it literally hits you in the face and yells "Surpriiiiise!" And then, all of a sudden, your whole life is invaded by the unknown; the unforeseen; the new. Surprise throws us off balance. Regaining balance is often a struggle as you need to adjust and find new ways to cope—and this is how you uncover a huge personal potential that would have never been discovered or put to use in normal circumstances.

Now think about a moment of surprise in your life. Ask yourself: do I like surprises? Do I try to avoid them—even if I was not aware of it until now? What is it that I like about surprises—the thrill, the escape from predictability? Or what is it that I don't like—to be thrown off-balance?

Surprise helps us grow, develop, and mature as human beings. Take this thought with you and maybe store it somewhere safe in your mind. And when the unpredictable strikes again, take a deep breath, let the initial emotional wave move past you, maybe take a pen in your hand and let a piece of paper do the magic of re-centering your new self.

Close your eyes and immerse yourself in the moment you want to recreate. Pick up all that comes to mind—colors, sounds, people, smells, tastes, dreams, emotions—then take a pen and start expressing them in writing. It doesn't matter how or where on the page. No two people express their emotions the same way. You could write single words or short lines, poem-like clusters, or, if inspired, you could write as you would in a diary! Summon your memories, relive the moment in your mind, and let it pour out on the pages.

_____

_____

_____

_____

_____

_____

_____

_____

_____

_____

_____

_____

Is the defining moment you chose for this chapter linked to color? To shape? To textures of any kind? This is where it can all be recreated. Use whatever tools you like: colored pencils, crayons, fabrics, photos, clippings, anything that you feel can help you express your emotions linked to this defining moment. Don't let your mind dictate what looks good or not. That's not the point. The point is to obtain an expression of your inner landscape connected to the moment you chose.

Color this mandala in the shade(s) that best represent your defining moment. Don't feel compelled to go for the most conventional color. Make the choice that feels most genuine by allowing yourself to pick the color(s) you feel drawn to.

chapter 8

Love

Name of Event: _____

Age When Event Occurred: _____

About Love

....

"How are you, Love?"

"Whole and free."

It is not easy to write in a rational, technical manner about love; that is because love grows out of the maze of our living, out of our encounters and experiences, and it fills and binds together this intricate and unpredictable fabric called life. That is why we think love can best be told by stories. After all, some of the greatest stories of all time are love stories. Let us begin our introduction to love with a story.

There was once a little girl. Very early in her life, at about the time when she began her process of separation and self-discovery, she experienced the confusing difficulty to connect the profound and intense feelings she had deep inside with objects or subjects of the outside world. She felt a place in her chest that would produce the most amazing sensations and yet she didn't know what caused them; because, as she looked outside at her parents or siblings or friends, none of them seemed to be the source of her inner emotional music.

As time went by and the mind of the little girl failed to establish a correspondence between her feelings and the outside world, she reached the belief that her feelings were inappropriate and so she failed to create a communication channel for her emotions to come out and be expressed. She only put out what her surroundings taught her would be appropriate and expected: a hug for her mother, a solicitous attitude toward her friends, a wide and bright smile at the family dinner table; and yet none of these felt like they should have. They didn't have the warm, all-embracing, all-giving, nurturing quality of her early feelings.

What the little girl didn't know was that what she initially felt was unconditional, unseparated love. Before the process of parental separation when she perceived no difference between herself and the world, she was just allowing love to manifest itself freely through her, directed at everything and at nothing in particular. After the inevitable process of separation, her inability to find ways to direct her feelings to outside subjects made her suppress the source of her beautiful inner life. And so, from a source of love, she became a source of appropriate, yet shallow behavior. A situation her mind could cope with. But not her soul, as she felt a void and a lack of meaning in her life that she would secretly attempt to heal by sometimes whispering out, with no one hearing—"I love you"; and wondering what that really was: love. She had some memories of her initial emotions and feelings, yet she felt like she needed to find a recipient, a cup to pour her love into.

And so, life set out to push and help the little girl lift the lid off her heart and let the music be heard and poured out again. First, she got married. Then, she had children. Life brought her closer and closer back to that place where love dwelled inside of her. And yet, neither her marriage, nor her husband or her babies, whom she loved dearly to the best of her abilities at that time, could fill up the void. From time to time, late at night, she would still whisper "I love you" and craved to understand what that meant. And of course, life listened. Life continued to happen, produce change, and expose the little girl, now a fully-grown woman, to events that would eventually teach her what love was.

Now, as you probably have noticed, as a rule love stories are not easy stories. And that is because love has the quality of surprise to it to put us in a new, unpredictable place and to make us open up, even if unwillingly, to others. Why unwillingly? Because every good love story, one that leaves great and enduring teachings, happens in adverse circumstances. It forces us to face difficult options, to question our reality with both our mind and heart, and decide which one to follow. If you have ever been in a situation like this, you know how hard it is to decide what and who is right. Those who teach us about love have this amazing power to enter the most secluded and vulnerable parts of our souls and open the path back to love—and to ourselves.

It was no different for our heroine. The man she met was never meant to stay in her life. They met twice. The forced split caused by severe circumstances was a very tough experience, yet it was precisely this meeting and this man's meteoric presence in her life that made her plunge into the deepest corners of herself and fuel her to find her way back to love. She became aware that love had always been with her, resembling a tree: with firm roots in her heart and growing out and all around her, as much and as far as she allowed it to grow. Every person, situation, and being in her life contributed to nurture and make her tree of love grow. This man helped her find the root of love in her heart again, but it was up to her to live her life and make it grow.

For the first time in her adult years and after a long period where she had experienced the full emotional spectrum—from deep sadness to anger to shame to joy to trust to fear—the woman became aware that her love was enough, that the fact that she loved was more fulfilling than being loved. That she had lived, known and therefore *had* love forever, with herself, no matter who life would allow to stay with her or not. It was love that taught her forgiveness; it was love that healed sadness and anger; and it was love that brought about detachment. She knew she had the power to let go and finally allow freedom to herself and to others, because she no longer depended on others to bring about her happiness, joy, and love.

If there is one thing that this story is trying to tell us, it is the fact that we should not be afraid to admit what we feel—or don't feel. This is the first step. It is the way we can open the door to the possibility of discovery. Maybe you are one of those people who still wonder about what love is. So, wonder! Invite the answers in, and be prepared to be brave and live through what your future has to offer.

We live in an age where everyone wants to understand, decipher, talk about, discover, live, and breathe love. Love is the new Holy Grail, the ultimate purpose of our lives, the final destination of a fierce quest. Many of us have discovered the luring promise of love in delivering the elusive answer to the eternal question:

"Why am I here?"

"To love," would be the answer.

Love promises purpose, sense, fulfilment, a way out of the maddening *why?* of our existence. However, in all our encounters there were only very few people who were frank and bold enough to ask the question, "What is love?" And this question came in a context where love, the way this or that particular person understood and lived it, *did not* provide the answer. Did not offer the craved-for sense of purpose. People weren't even sure what they felt was actually love. Why?

Because in our desire to find love, we have used its name to designate emotions and feelings that feel nice, or good, or that uplift us in some way or make us feel affectionate or passionate or attached to something or someone. People say "love" to describe how they feel about many things in many ways. There is such an extensive variety when it comes to love, so many angles and degrees and shades of it, that maybe the best way to look at love would be to see it as a ladder that offers us a wider and more complete perspective as we climb each ring; or as a big puzzle that we slowly put together as our lives unfold and offer us various experiences; or yes, as a tree, like the love tree in our story.

As we live our lives, love is always present. However, we perceive only as much of it as our experience allows. We need to live, to experience life as a child, friend, pupil, pet owner, parent, brother or sister, lover, husband and wife, you name it, to amass experience after experience where love manifests itself.

The funny thing about love is that sometimes it doesn't feel like love at all or it feels like it is lacking altogether in situations where it should be present. We know of a man who was terrified to realize, when asked to bring back loving memories of his sister when they were children, that he could come up with none. All he could remember were either neutral or bad memories and he finally had to face up to the brutal and not-at-all-easy to admit truth that he didn't feel like he loved his sister. When investigating further, he realized that he had difficulties entering situations where love would manifest overtly. He was afraid of love. It was not that he wasn't capable of it, he was running away from it. That was his truth. Why? Because he subconsciously knew that love would make him vulnerable and would force him to go in and face his reasons for shame, sadness, and anger.

Now we have come to the point where we can see that love is linked with all emotions: fear, sadness, surprise, joy, happiness, anger, shame, and trust, to take just those that we briefly covered so far. Let's be playful for a bit and imagine ourselves as cups; emotionally, life fills us with all sorts of feelings and emotions. The first ones, those that we experience as children, go to the bottom of the cup and form our emotional foundation. And then, as life goes by, our cup continues to fill and creates the most unique emotional configurations. However, the only way our cup can be truly filled is by making sure there is something poured in that has the fluid quality of water—it permeates every corner and leaves no hole or empty place—that would be love.

Wise men say our lives are given to us to teach us love. We all enter life and subtly choose the experiences which have the best potential to make us learn what love is.

So, what is love?

From a scientific perspective, this is a difficult question. For one, there is no unanimous consensus on whether love is an emotion or a feeling. The simply-defined difference between an emotion and a feeling is their endurance in time. An emotion is mostly short-lived; a feeling lasts.

Let's take the example of sadness; you may experience a short period of sadness when seeing a friend cry. But that sadness goes away soon after you engage in other activities, leaving room for other emotions. In this particular case, sadness manifests as an emotion. However, when sadness is associated with a loss that made a big impact in your life, it will likely last longer and develop into a feeling.

It's the same with love. We may say "Awww, I love this picture!" in front of an image that triggers an affectionate response. However, this emotion does not last. The cute content of the picture usually does not stay with us for too long. In this case, we would refer to love as an emotion. When the emotion lasts, develops, grows, and expands, it turns into the feeling of love. This would be the more technical definition of love, for those of you who prefer a more rational approach.

But past any attempt at a definition, remember that love does the magic of taking us deep and far into our secret vulnerable places. It is the water that fills up our cup no matter what that cup holds, infiltrating any opening. That is what makes love so important. It makes us whole again.

Close your eyes and immerse yourself in the moment you want to recreate. Pick up all that comes to mind—colors, sounds, people, smells, tastes, dreams, emotions—then take a pen and start expressing them in writing. It doesn't matter how or where on the page. No two people express their emotions the same way. You could write single words or short lines, poem-like clusters, or, if inspired, you could write as you would in a diary! Summon your memories, relive the moment in your mind, and let it pour out on the pages.

_____

_____

_____

_____

_____

_____

_____

_____

_____

_____

_____

_____

_____

_____

Is the defining moment you chose for this chapter linked to color? To shape? To textures of any kind? This is where it can all be recreated. Use whatever tools you like: colored pencils, crayons, fabrics, photos, clippings, anything that you feel can help you express your emotions linked to this defining moment. Don't let your mind dictate what looks good or not. That's not the point. The point is to obtain an expression of your inner landscape connected to the moment you chose.

Color this mandala in the shade(s) that best represent your defining moment. Don't feel compelled to go for the most conventional color. Make the choice that feels most genuine by allowing yourself to pick the color(s) you feel drawn to.

Instead of Ending

....

At this point, it is our hope that you own something you can call your book, and that this book helped you write yourself and recreate the essential moments of your life. You can tenderly put it in your bookcase; you can show it to your friends, family, and everyone who is important to you. Remember to open it from time to time. Read what you wrote, analyze what you draw or colored. See if there is any change in the way you feel about your eight defining moments.

This book was also a journey into the intricate and fascinating world of human emotions; of your emotions and feelings. Many of us master knowledge in various fields and are so good at using our bodies and our brains, but our overall level of literacy is not so high when it comes to matters of the heart and soul. We *know* we feel, but often we are not so sure about *what* we feel and *why* we feel it. And then, we may have difficulties on how to *act* on our feelings and emotions.

Coming to terms with our emotions is a lifelong journey. We cannot do it without plunging into the intimate depths of our souls, living and feeling, and then living some more and feeling some more; and, in the process, never forgetting that emotions are the best teachers and wise mirrors of who we were at a certain point in our lives.

What do joy and happiness teach us? To aspire—either to inner balance and peace or to external objectives, whichever of the two are the right paths of our lives in a given moment.

What does anger teach us? To fight injustice in a just way; to correctly identify and state our reasons for being angry; to open up and let that fire out to cause positive change.

What does sadness teach us? How to find our soul, how to go as deep into our hearts as possible. How to handle loss; how not to identify ourselves with our loss.

What does fear teach us? To reassess the idea of danger. To identify our reasons for fear and face them when the time is right. To go past our fear-induced limitations into a new territory where our greatest gifts and opportunities lay.

What does trust teach us? To work with ourselves and learn how to trust all over again—starting with ourselves.

What does shame teach us? To identify our perfect projection of ourselves, see where it clashes with our reality, learn what is true and what is fake, and then act on it or let go and accept ourselves.

What does surprise teach us? That there is always something that we don't know. That our own personal universe is infinite and surprise is here to expand our perception of it and make us adjust, learn, and grow in the process.

What does love teach us? That we can be whole again. That the process of separation has done its job of making us aware that we all connect and that there is no need and never was a need for separation. The story has come full circle.

A book is a magical thing. When it is born, a new reality is born along with it, carrying so much potential. We are happy to have been on this journey with you. Always remember, you are still writing the amazing book of your life!

With love,

The Authors